THE KIDS' GUIDE TO STAYING AWESOME AND IN CONTROL

of related interest

The Red Beast
Controlling Anger in Children with Asperger's Syndrome
K.I. Al-Ghani
Illustrated by Haitham Al-Ghani
ISBN 978 1 84310 943 3
eISBN 978 1 84642 848 7

The Panicosaurus
Managing Anxiety in Children Including Those with Asperger Syndrome
K.I. Al-Ghani
Illustrated by Haitham Al-Ghani
ISBN 978 1 84905 356 3
eISBN 978 0 85700 706 3

The Disappointment Dragon
Learning to cope with disappointment (for all children and dragon
tamers, including those with Asperger Syndrome)
K.I. Al-Ghani
Illustrated by Haitham Al-Ghani
ISBN 978 1 84905 432 4
eISBN 978 0 85700 780 3

THE KIDS' GUIDE TO STAYING
AWESOME
AND IN CONTROL

Simple Stuff to Help Children
Regulate their Emotions and Senses

LAUREN BRUKNER
ILLUSTRATED BY APSLEY

Jessica Kingsley *Publishers*
London and Philadelphia

This book, and all of the strategies provided, are not intended to provide medical or diagnostic information. This book is not a replacement for occupational therapy, physical therapy, vision therapy, speech therapy, or any other specific services your child may need. If your child has a suspected or diagnosed medical condition, speak with your paediatrician before engaging in any suggested exercises, or trying any tools or strategies, to ensure that they are safe and appropriate.

First published in 2014
by Jessica Kingsley Publishers
73 Collier Street
London N1 9BE, UK
and
400 Market Street, Suite 400
Philadelphia, PA 19106, USA

www.jkp.com

Copyright © Lauren Brukner 2014
Illustrations copyright © Apsley 2014

Library of Congress Cataloging in Publication Data
Brukner, Lauren.
 The kids' guide to staying awesome and in control : simple stuff to help children regulate their emotions and senses / Lauren Brukner ; illustrated by Apsley.
    pages cm
 Includes bibliographical references.
 Audience: Age 7-14.
 ISBN 978-1-84905-997-8 (alk. paper)
 1. Self-control in children--Juvenile literature. 2. Emotions in children--Juvenile literature. 3. Child psychology--Juvenile literature. I. Apsley, illustrator. II. Title.
 BF723.S25B78 2014
 155.4'182--dc23
                          2013050308

British Library Cataloguing in Publication Data
A CIP catalogue record for this book is available from the British Library

ISBN 978 1 84905 997 8
eISBN 978 0 85700 962 3

Printed and bound in the United States

Dedicated to my husband and three children, whom I love more than the moon and back.

Contents

PART 2: FOR ADULTS

PART 1

FOR KIDS

Hey Kids, Let Me Tell You A Little About Me and This Book!

My name is Lauren, and I am an occupational therapist. I spend my days working with kids, and I *love* my job! I help students of different ages feel calm in their bodies and minds in tons of different ways.

Can I tell you a secret? When I was a kid, I often had trouble paying attention in class, saying what was bothering me, and calming down when I got sad, angry, or frustrated (which, honestly, was quite often). Being at school was often hard, being at home was often hard, and I often felt like I did not have control over my own life. I think that having those difficulties made me grow up and want to have a job that would help children not only know *what* or *how* they were feeling, but also give them the power and control to *change* or *improve* that feeling through exercises, tools, or other strategies (big words, I know, but don't worry—I will explain more later).

I have worked hard to put in all of the different strategies and tools that have worked for me and the kids that I work with, as well as my own three children at home, in order to help you, amazing readers, feel just right and in control of your body, feelings, and actions. This project has made me super-excited and I can't wait to share my tool box with you!

Lauren

CHAPTER 1

Label That Feeling!

In this chapter, I am introducing you to three very important (but maybe, very strange-sounding, at first) feelings that we will be working with throughout this book.

Almost any type of *physical* (in your body) or *emotional* (in your mind or heart) feeling that you may have can really fall into one of these three categories.

They are (drum-roll, please...): **Slow and Tired**, **Fast and Emotional**, and **Fast and Wiggly**.

When you are calm, you feel **Just Right**. Being **Just Right** is *peaceful*. Your breathing is slow and even. You feel happy. You can pay attention to parents, teachers, and friends. You don't feel angry. You don't feel too tired or too wiggly.

When you are **Slow and Tired**, your body feels very *tired*. It may be hard for you to sit up on the floor, or even on a chair. Your eyelids may feel droopy, your arms and legs may feel too heavy to move. It may be really hard to pay attention to your teacher or your parents, or even to talk to or play with your friends. Your movements may be very slow, or they may be super-fast (to try to wake yourself up).

When you see this ☺💤 symbol next to pictures, strategies, or tools in this book, this means that the strategy, exercise, or tool that is being talked about can help when you are feeling **Slow and Tired**.

Sometimes, you may feel **Fast and Emotional**. Your heart beats too fast, noises can sound too loud, objects you see can be too bright. Your brain may be thinking about thoughts that are making you feel *stressed* or *worried*. Your body moves *super-fast*, as if you are escaping from a real danger. You may look hyper, but something that you are thinking about is what is truly bothering you.

When you see this ⊗ ☁ symbol next to pictures, strategies, or tools in this book, this means that the strategy, exercise, or tool that is being talked about can help when you are feeling **Fast and Emotional**.

When you are feeling **Fast and Wiggly**, your body feels like it needs to move. There is *too* much energy that needs to be let out! You may have a hard time focusing on your teachers, parents, or even friends, and can *even* have difficulty playing with them the right way sometimes (for example, you might accidentally knock over the block tower because you need to move your body more than your friends while building).

When you see this 😃 symbol next to pictures, strategies, or tools in this book, this means that the strategy, exercise, or tool that is being talked about can help when you are feeling **Fast and Wiggly**.

Almost everybody feels at least *two* of those feelings every day (yes, including adults!). Thank goodness, we also have lots of *great* feelings to balance the not-so-great ones out. The trick is: knowing what to do with those troublesome **Slow and Tired**, **Fast and Emotional**, and **Fast and Wiggly** feelings when they come up!

So, here's the thing. Our bodies are *always* trying to get to a state of **Just Right**. As a kid, you may need some help getting your bodies to feel that way. That is where (drum-roll please!) these amazingly-awesome body breaks, strategies, and tools come in.

CHAPTER 2

Let's Learn the HOW of Using Anywhere Body Breaks!

We have reviewed what each feeling means. We know that it is normal to experience each and probably all of those feelings in any given day (remember, even your teachers and parents do, too!).

So, what can you do about it? Well, the first thing to try would be an **Anywhere Body Break**, of course!

Now, here is where I teach you what an **Anywhere Body Break** is, and the reasons behind *why* you would want to use these **Anywhere Body Breaks** in the first place!

(In my opinion, why bother doing exercises and strategies if you don't understand: (a) *what* they are, and (b) the science behind *why* they work? I know that *I* wouldn't want to…)

What is an "Anywhere Body Break," anyway?

An **Anywhere Body Break** is a "small movement" exercise that you can do *using your own body*. The reason I call it "small movement" is because you can do these exercises from a regular sitting or standing stance, without having to change your whole body position. They work really well, and the great news is that you can use them without disrupting what you were doing to either get a **tool** or take a **Big Break**. That means, you finish your work faster, become more focused, and get to spend more time doing the stuff you *want* to do!

(Psst! Hey, readers, this is important!): I must state now that you should *always, always, always* try using **Anywhere Body Breaks** as your first step in your quest to feeling **Just Right**.

So now we know what an Anywhere Body Break is, but *why* and *how* do they work? What makes them so great?

★ **Reason 1:** You only need your own body (not another person or a squeeze ball, just yourself!).

★ **Reason 2:** You can do them *anywhere* (and I mean anywhere; the supermarket, recess, gym, a championship baseball game…).

★ **Reason 3:** They are so "not obvious" that nobody can tell that you are even doing them.

★ **Reason 4:** They are meant to be *calming* and *focusing*, so they are super awesome before an exam, or if you are feeling stressed, angry or upset.

★ **Reason 5:** A lot of these movement exercises include a pattern involving a cool scientific term called **"crossing midline"**—when a body part on one side crosses over to the other side. This movement causes one half of your brain to talk to the other half, which helps you *focus* when you need to.

★ **Reason 6:** Many of these exercises involve using *deep pressure* or **"proprioceptive input"** (letting your body know where it is in space). So, as long as you do these breaks slowly and with firm pressure, you can do these exercises whether you are **Slow and Tired**, **Fast and Emotional**, or **Fast and Wiggly** in order to feel in control!

OK, guys. We are ready to explore our (drum roll, please) **Anywhere Body Break** choices. Follow the directions, and see how your body feels after each one. Think back to learning how to label your feelings. This can help you determine which exercises can help you to feel **Just Right**. Remember, look for the helpful symbols next to each tool that match each feeling, for a quick reminder of how that tool would help (for example, looking at the 😑💤 😦 symbol next to the **Arm-Pretzel**, you can quickly see that it would help you if you are feeling **Slow and Tired** or **Fast and Wiggly**).

Lauren's Self-Regulation Menu of AWESOME Anywhere Body Break "Appetizer" Choices

ARM-PRETZEL

Hold for ten seconds.

This exercise has you **cross midline**, which can really help you focus if you are feeling **Slow and Tired**, or **Fast and Wiggly**.

Directions

★ Arms like a seal.

★ Cross arms.

★ Touch palms.

★ Interlace fingers.

★ Twist arms to chest.

Slow and Tired

Fast and Emotional

Fast and Wiggly

BUBBLE BREATH

Breathe in for five seconds, out for five seconds.

This is a good exercise to do, whether you are feeling: **Slow and Tired**, **Fast and Emotional**, or **Fast and Wiggly**. Getting oxygen to your brain can help you think better and make smarter choices, as well.

Directions

★ Imagine you have a wand of bubbles. When you breathe out, be careful not to pop it!

★ Place one flat palm on your heart, one flat palm on your belly.

★ Breathe in through your nose and hold your breath for five seconds.

★ Breathe out a large "bubble" through pursed lips, blow out and hold for five seconds.

Slow and Tired   Fast and Emotional   Fast and Wiggly

GIVE MYSELF A HUG

This can help you feel where your belly and back are by giving you **proprioceptive input**, which can then help calm you down whether you are feeling **Fast and Emotional** or **Fast and Wiggly**.

It can also wake you up if you are feeling **Slow and Tired**. This exercise also has you **cross midline**, which can really help you focus if you are feeling **Slow and Tired**, or **Fast and Wiggly**.

Directions

★ Cross your arms in front of you, far enough to bring your palms almost to your sides.

★ Squeeze your arms or sides firmly, and hold for five to ten seconds.

Slow and Tired

Fast and Emotional

Fast and Wiggly

ARM MASSAGE

Firmly squeeze your arms, from your wrists to your shoulders, or from your shoulders to your wrists.

This can help you feel where your arms are by giving you **proprioceptive input**, which can then help calm you down whether you are feeling **Fast and Emotional** or **Fast and Wiggly**. It can also wake you up if you are feeling **Slow and Tired**.

(Alternative: To improve focus, cross wrists and squeeze them at the same time, going up the arms together!)

Directions

★ Starting at the wrist or shoulder, squeeze firmly.

★ Do this motion, going up or down the arm five to ten times.

★ Do the same motions to the other arm.

Alternative:

★ Cross wrists, squeeze wrists at the same time.

★ Go up and down the arms five to ten times.

Slow and Tired   Fast and Emotional   Fast and Wiggly

HAND MASSAGE

Using the thumb of one hand, press firmly around the palm of the other hand.

This can help you feel where your hands are by giving you **proprioceptive input**, which can then help calm you down whether you are feeling **Fast and Emotional** or **Fast and Wiggly**. It can also wake you up if you are feeling **Slow and Tired**.

Directions

★ Starting with one thumb, push along the palm of the other hand five to ten times.

★ Repeat with the other palm.

Slow and Tired   Fast and Emotional   Fast and Wiggly

FINGER PULL

Lock your two hands together by your fingertips, and hold for ten seconds.

This exercise can really help you feel where your fingers and hands are by giving you **proprioceptive input**, which can then help calm you down whether you are feeling **Fast and Emotional** or **Fast and Wiggly**.

I often tell kids that I work with: "Put all of your bad feelings into your finger pull, and keep pulling until you pull the feeling right out of your body!" Pull really hard until you want to stop. Give it a try, I bet this becomes one of your favorites!

Directions

★ Put one hand palm up, one hand palm down (both facing each other).

★ Touch fingertips together (except thumbs), and pull them apart as hard as you can.

★ Hold for as long as your body needs to (five to ten seconds, at least).

Slow and Tired   Fast and Emotional   Fast and Wiggly

PALM PUSH

Push your palms together, and hold for five to ten seconds.

This exercise can help you feel where your fingers and hands are by giving you **proprioceptive input**, which can then help calm you down whether you are feeling **Fast and Emotional** or **Fast and Wiggly**. It can also wake you up if you are feeling **Slow and Tired**.

Directions

★ Face your palms together.

★ Push them firmly together, and hold this position for five to ten seconds.

Slow and Tired

Fast and Emotional

Fast and Wiggly

SEAT PUSH-UP

Sit on the floor with your legs crossed or in a chair with your feet flat. Push on the floor or on the chair with flat palms. Count for five to ten seconds.

This can help you feel where your fingers and hands are by giving you **proprioceptive input**, which can then help calm you down whether you are feeling **Fast and Emotional** or **Fast and Wiggly**.

This is a great exercise if you are feeling **Slow and Tired**.

(Note: Make sure not to lift your body too far off the floor, or you are not doing this exercise correctly—you may hurt yourself or become *more* **Fast and Wiggly**, or **Slow and Tired**!)

Directions

★ Sit with your feet crossed or in a chair with your feet flat on the floor.

★ Push your bottom up from either the floor, or from the seat of the chair with flat palms.

★ Hold for five to ten seconds.

Slow and Tired   Fast and Emotional   Fast and Wiggly

COUNT TO TEN

Stop what you are doing or saying, and count quietly or in your head to ten.

This is a good strategy to use when you are feeling **Fast and Emotional**, or even when you are **Fast and Wiggly**.

Stopping yourself by counting can help you think more clearly before you act, while allowing you to make better choices in what you say and what you do.

Directions

★ STOP!

★ Give yourself a reminder: "Count," "Ten," or another familiar and quick thought that you practice and can go back to quickly in situations that feel hard.

★ Use your fingers, a timer, a clock, or quietly count in your head one, two, three…

Slow and Tired   Fast and Emotional   Fast and Wiggly

CHAPTER 3

Let's Learn the HOW of Using Tools!

So, you chose your "appetizer" breaks and strategies. Many times, these breaks and strategies give kids just enough movement or help so they are able to do work they need to do or play with friends or spend time with family members. However, there are times when these **Anywhere Body Breaks** are not enough. But why, you may ask. And what are "**tools**," anyway? Let's explore, shall we?

We just learned how amazing Anywhere Body Breaks are! Why would they not work for me all the time?

Examples of times that this may happen are when…

★ **Reason 1:** You did not sleep well the night before.

★ **Reason 2:** You did not eat a good meal.

★ **Reason 3:** You are feeling *extra* **Slow and Tired**, **Fast and Emotional**, or **Fast and Wiggly**.

If so, the next step would be to use a **tool**:

But, hey, first and foremost, what is a tool?

Great question! A tool is something *extrinsic* to your body (that means it is not a part of your body). People in different professions use tools in different ways; for example, a construction worker or a handyman may use a hammer to push in a nail to keep two boards together. He uses the hammer to get the job done. While we will *not* use hammers, our tools that we will discuss help us in a similar way.

You will learn how to use specific tools to help you feel just right in your body and mind so that you can do *your job* of being a kid both well *and* happily. (Hey, I remember being a kid—it wasn't that long ago! You have a lot of different jobs, and it is not always easy… I get it.)

(Note: Choosing the right or wrong tool can either make you feel better or worse. A lot depends on the choices that you make.)

OK, you are now ready for the next step. Let's learn *how* to use **tools** to feel just right (and to use them *correctly*, I might add). Just remember, look for the symbols next to each tool that match each feeling, for a quick reminder of how that tool would help (for example, looking at the ☺😴 symbol next to the Back Jack Chair, you can quickly see that it would help you if you are feeling **Slow and Tired**).

Lauren's Self-Regulation Menu of AWESOME Tool "Main Dish" Choices

NOISE-REDUCING HEADPHONES

Use these if there is too much noise around you and you need to focus. Headphones may also help if you are feeling **Fast and Emotional**, and need to block out the noise around you to feel calm. Sometimes, when your body feels **Fast and Wiggly**, wearing headphones can help you focus on your work or walk around a noisy place and help you feel **Just Right**.

Slow and Tired

Fast and Emotional

Fast and Wiggly

CUSHION

A *wedge* cushion is especially good if you have trouble sitting upright. It forces you to sit up straighter. A *disc* cushion is circular. Both are filled with air, and cause you to constantly shift your body around, keeping you moving. Some disc cushions come with bumps, and some cushions come without bumps. The cushions that come with bumps can even give you something to feel with your hands when you are sitting on it. Whether you are feeling the bumps with your hands or your legs, you are giving your body more of what therapists call **tactile input** (through the sense of touch).

Give them a try if you are feeling **Slow and Tired** or **Fast and Wiggly**.

Tip: If you're in a pinch, and don't have one of these special pillows nearby, you can use a regular pillow, or fold up a sweatshirt or puffy coat. This is a less obvious yet very effective way to use a cushion!

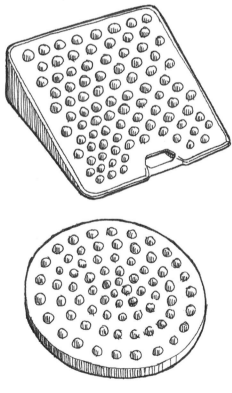

Slow and Tired   Fast and Emotional   Fast and Wiggly

FIDGET

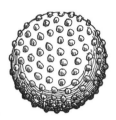

A fidget is a ball or hand-held object that remains in your hand, to be "fidgeted" with.

Here are a few simple but very important rules:

1. Fidgets are not toys and should not be played with!

2. Your eyes must always be on the teacher or speaker (or work you are doing), not on the fidget.

3. The fidget should not leave your hands.

4. *Textured fidgets* (bumps, etc.) are good if you are feeling **Slow and Tired**. *Firm fidgets* (filled with sand, flour, beans, etc.) are good if you are feeling either **Slow and Tired**, **Fast and Emotional**, or **Fast and Wiggly**. Just like the finger-pull, put the feeling into using the fidget and it will work a lot better!

Tip: If you're in a pinch, and don't have an actual fidget in your possession but do own self-adhesive Velcro, try attaching this to the bottom of a desk, the bottom of a chair, the floor, or the back of a notebook. This will act as a textured fidget (and only you would know about it!). It is a less obvious yet very effective way to use a fidget (especially if you don't trust yourself enough not to follow the rules listed above).

Slow and Tired   Fast and Emotional   Fast and Wiggly

WEIGHTED LAP/NECK PAD

You can either wear this on your lap or around your neck.

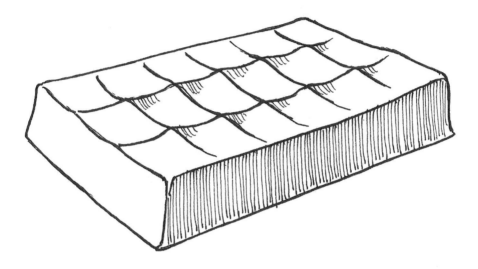

This is a good tool to use if you are feeling **Fast and Emotional** or **Fast and Wiggly**, because it provides you with **proprioceptive input** (letting your body know where it is in space).

Slow and Tired   Fast and Emotional   Fast and Wiggly

WEIGHTED VEST

This tool is similar to the weighted lap pad, but this is worn on your body (either over or under your clothing). It feels like a hug!

I recommend (and this is only my recommendation as an occupational therapist) that this should be worn for no more than twenty minutes at a time, and its weight should not exceed five percent of your own body weight (ask an occupational therapist for help with this!).

This is a good tool to use if you are feeling **Fast and Emotional** or **Fast and Wiggly**, because it provides you with **proprioceptive input** (letting your body know where it is in space).

Slow and Tired

Fast and Emotional

Fast and Wiggly

COMPRESSION VEST/CLOTHING

These types of clothing are made up of tight material which provides that "magical" **proprioceptive input** to your body (especially your shoulders and waist). It feels very calming, *like getting a hug.*

You can wear this all day. Slip on a vest if you are feeling **Slow and Tired**, **Fast and Emotional**, or **Fast and Wiggly**.

Know the day may be a tough one (long day, big test, difficult time the night before, etc.)? You can also wear compression clothing (e.g. a compression T-shirt) underneath your clothes to help you feel in control all day long.

Slow and Tired · Fast and Emotional · Fast and Wiggly

ROCKING CHAIR

Rock *slowly and rhythmically* if you feel **Fast and Emotional** or **Fast and Wiggly**.

Ask to sit on this during reading or when your teacher is teaching on the rug, or at home during reading or another activity where you have to sit for a long period of time.

| Slow and Tired | Fast and Emotional | Fast and Wiggly |

BACK JACK CHAIR

Use this tool on the rug if you are feeling **Slow and Tired**. This can help you sit up better and pay attention, because it will give you something to lean on, as well as that **proprioceptive input** to your back that we have been talking about.

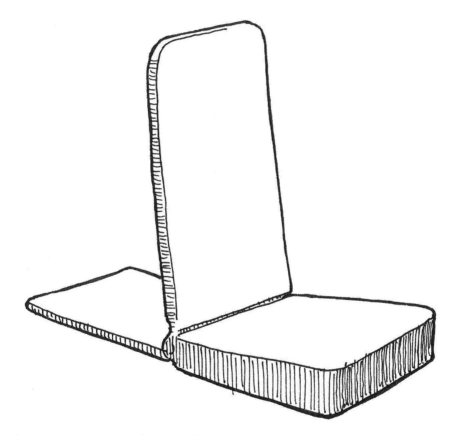

(Alternative: Don't have a back jack chair? Find a wall or long bookcase on the rug, and take large sofa cushions or pillows and sit up against this instead!)

Slow and Tired   Fast and Emotional   Fast and Wiggly

DESK CORREL

Do you become distracted by people, posters, or other things that you can see when you are at your desk working? If so, you may want to give this a try!

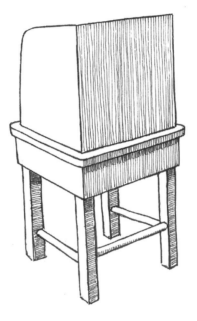

This tool can be bought from a store. It is basically a piece of material that is used to block off your workspace.

You can make your own out of a big folder, or a few folders stacked next to each other. To use this tool the right way, take responsibility for yourself and sit nicely on your chair—don't peer over the top, or what is the point of using this?

Tip: This works really well with noise-reducing headphones, especially when the classroom or workspace is loud! (Can your house get noisy? Mine can!)

MANIPULATIVES

What are manipulatives?

Examples of manipulatives include: stacking unifix cubes, lacing beads, and connecting Lego bricks.

They can be a powerful tool to use when you feel *very* **Fast and Emotional** and need a busy break. A busy break keeps your body and mind occupied when you are feeling a strong emotion. Using manipulatives can also help when you are feeling **Fast and Wiggly** (when you really need something to keep your hands busy, and a fidget or an **Anywhere Body Break** appetizer choice is not enough).

Slow and Tired   Fast and Emotional   Fast and Wiggly

Here's the rub: since a lot of these choices can be used as toys, when you choose this as a "main dish" exercise, you must make sure that you are using these manipulatives the right way.

There are similar "rules" with these as with fidgets:

1. Manipulatives are not toys and should not be played with!

2. Know yourself as a learner:

   - If you are using this when you are feeling **Fast and Emotional**, will you be able to stop using this when asked by the adult?

   - If you are using this when you are feeling **Fast and Wiggly**, are you the type of learner who can listen *best* to the teacher while building/manipulating the tool? Will you know to put your eyes up during times that your teacher is showing the class important information that needs to be looked at?

   - Be honest with yourself—if the answer is no, there are so many other choices in this manual to try. Be proud of yourself for being flexible.

3. The manipulatives should not leave your hands or area of work (e.g. desk, workspace).

GUM

The act of chewing gum is a good way to stay calm and focused—but please check with a grown-up for permission to chew gum!

Since the act of chewing gum (especially if it is a little firm) requires a lot of hard jaw work, this provides your body with more of that amazing **proprioceptive input** (especially in your mouth and to your facial muscles, too).

This tool can help wake you up if you are feeling **Slow and Tired**, and calm you down if you are feeling **Fast and Emotional** or **Fast and Wiggly**.

*Tip: Minty flavors will wake you up even more so they are good if you are feeling **Slow and Tired** (for example, peppermint and spearmint). Fruity flavors are more calming.*

Slow and Tired   Fast and Emotional   Fast and Wiggly

WATER BOTTLE WITH A STRAW

This tool works in a similar way to using gum. Drinking water through a straw can really help keep you feeling calm and focused, especially if the straw has a lot of "resistance"—that is, your mouth has to work hard to get the water through.

Since the act of sucking water through the straw (especially if it has a lot of resistance) requires a lot of hard sucking, this provides your body with more of that amazing **proprioceptive input** (especially in your mouth and to your facial muscles, too).

This tool can help wake you up if you are feeling **Slow and Tired**, and calm you down if you are feeling **Fast and Emotional** or **Fast and Wiggly**.

Slow and Tired   Fast and Emotional   Fast and Wiggly

CRUNCHY SNACKS/SOUR OR SPICY FLAVORS/COLD OR FROZEN FOODS

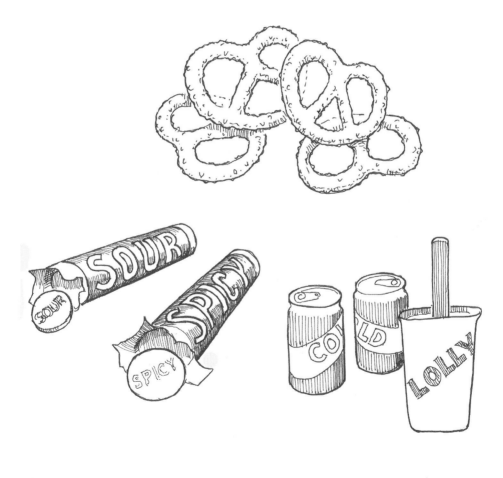

All of these types of foods are very alerting to your body, so you can give these a try if you are feeling **Slow and Tired**.

Some examples are pretzels, sour flavored gum and frozen juice popsicles.

Slow and Tired   Fast and Emotional   Fast and Wiggly

CHAPTER 4

Let's Learn the HOW of Using Big Body Breaks!

Phew. OK. You have gotten to this page. It's a lot of information, I know. But hey, it's a lot of really helpful stuff, so bear with me, OK?

So we have covered a lot of ground at this point. We understand how to: label our feelings (remembering how, many times, we can feel a mixture of different states, such as **Fast and Emotional** and **Fast and Wiggly**), and choose appropriate **Anywhere Body Breaks** and **tools** to help us feel just right. We even understand the science behind why they work! We have learned how, many times, an **Anywhere Body Break** is enough to help us feel in control, but that sometimes we may need a **tool** to keep us happy, focused, and calm.

Everyone has those days where they need a little *extra*. That is where these **Big Body Breaks** come in.

In this chapter, let's explore (a) what a **Big Body Break** is, and (b) some simple rules to keep you doing these exercises correctly so that you feel great!

So, when would Anywhere Body Breaks and tools not be enough?

★ **Reason 1:** You did not sleep well the night before.

★ **Reason 2:** You did not eat a good meal.

★ **Reason 3:** You are feeling extra **Slow and Tired** or **Fast and Wiggly**, and need that extra movement to wake up or calm down.

★ **Reason 4:** You are feeling extra **Fast and Emotional**, and need to take some space or get out extra energy to feel in control.

Now would be the time to do some **Big Body Breaks**.

So, what is a Big Body Break?

A **Big Body Break** is a "large movement" exercise that you can do using your own body. The reason I call it "large movement" is because you usually have to do these exercises from a standing, belly-up, or belly-down stance, using big movements. You usually need a certain amount of free floor or wall space to do these exercises. You also need to leave, and sometimes disrupt, what you were doing (for example, go to a separate space in the classroom or hallway if you are in school, go into the hallway or more open space in your home). These exercises provide you with a ton of **proprioceptive input** and **crossing midline** elements, so they work really well and usually pretty quickly, too. That means, after you finish these exercises, you can easily come back to your work faster and more focused, and get to spend time doing the stuff you *want* to do!

Let's put **Big Body Breaks** in the "dessert" section of our self-regulation menu, because you don't need them all the time, but there *are* some times that you've just got to have one.

OK, so now you know *what* a **Big Body Break** is. There are some simple rules to follow to keep you doing them correctly, so that you get the most out of these exercises:

★ Rule 1: **Big Body Breaks** outside the classroom (or if you are at home, away from what you are doing) should last no more than two or three minutes. Use a timer to check yourself, or ask a helpful adult to assist in timing you.

  – Note: This is different from "taking space": needing time away safely from a situation that makes your body or mind feel extra **Fast and Emotional** (or even **Fast and Wiggly**, at times). You always need to get permission from an adult to take space, and this must be done in a safe manner, where grown-ups know exactly where you are and for how long you will be there.

Tip: You can even set up a safe spot in your classroom or your house. You can ask to put in tools or items that make you feel safe; for example, special fidgets, a weighted lap pad, noise-reducing headphones, markers/paper, a picture of family/ friends. This can always be a safe spot for you to go when you begin to feel **Fast and Emotional***, or* **Fast and Wiggly***, to try to "nip those feelings in the bud."*

★ Rule 2: **Big Body Breaks** that separate you from the classroom (or if you are at home, away from what you are doing) should not be an "excuse" to get out of class or away from your other responsibilities (I know, I sound like such a *grown-up*, but it's true!). If you need a break, ask your helpful grown-up if you can get a quick drink of water, stretch and come right back to what you were doing instead.

  – Note: If you take these Big Body Breaks when you need to, and do them the right way, you will really see that they work. Plus, you will show the grown-ups in your life that you are responsible, honest, and take responsibility for yourself, your learning, and your behavior! They may be so pleased with you that you may be surprised with occasional extra choice time or video game time, I don't know... (But I'm not making any promises, and hey, the ball is in *your* court!)

★ Rule 3: When you are doing these breaks, keep this in mind:

  – To feel more *energized*, make your movements quick (but *controlled*).

  – To feel more *calm*, go slowly and with more strength in your movements. This will give more **proprioceptive input** to your joints, which, as you know by now, is very calming.

Tip: I don't know how many times I have seen kids go out on **Big Body Breaks** *and just automatically go to either do* fast jumping jacks, or race down the hallway and do army crawls super-fast. (*Don't know what those are? Turn the next few pages, you are about to find out!*) Keep this in mind: Doing breaks *the right way* and at *the right speed* is just as important as choosing the *right type of exercise. I think that it's natural to want to just rush out of class or away from homework or chores and automatically do* **Big Body Breaks** *quickly without thinking.*

OK, we are ready to learn *how* to do **Big Body Breaks** to feel **Just Right** (and to do them correctly, I might add). Just remember, look for the helpful symbols next to each tool that match each feeling, for a quick reminder of how that tool would help (for example, looking at the 😑💤, 😠🌧 and ☺ symbols next to the **Wall Push**, you can quickly see that it would help you if you are feeling **Slow and Tired**, **Fast and Emotional**, or **Fast and Wiggly**).

Lauren's Self-Regulation Menu of AWESOME Big Body Break "Dessert" Choices

WALL PUSH

All you need for this exercise is a sturdy, blank wall.

With flat palms, and feet planted on the floor, push against the wall and hold this position for five to ten seconds.

This exercise provides **proprioceptive input** to your hands, arms, and legs, so can make you feel **Just Right** whether you are feeling **Slow and Tired**, **Fast and Emotional**, or **Fast and Wiggly**.

Slow and Tired   Fast and Emotional   Fast and Wiggly

ARMY CRAWL

For this exercise, you need enough free floor space to move around. Lie on your belly, with your palms flat on the floor. Push your body forward using only your palms.

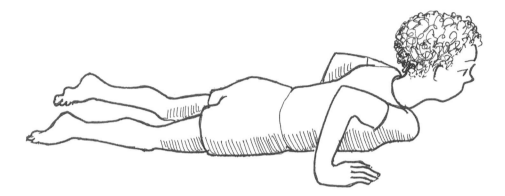

This exercise provides **proprioceptive input** to your belly, back, arms, and legs, so can make you feel **Just Right** whether you are feeling **Slow and Tired**, **Fast and Emotional**, or **Fast and Wiggly**.

Tip: You can reach your right arm towards the left side of the floor while crawling, and vice versa. By doing this you are **crossing midline** *(remember that?), when one body part crosses to the other part of the body. This movement causes one side of your brain to talk to the other side, which helps you focus when you need to.*

Slow and Tired

Fast and Emotional

Fast and Wiggly

CRAB WALK

For this exercise, you need enough free floor space to move around. Walk on your palms and feet with your belly facing up. Keep your back as straight as you can.

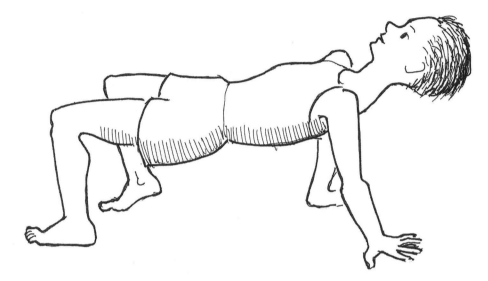

This exercise provides **proprioceptive input** to your belly, back, arms, and legs, and is especially helpful when you are feeling **Slow and Tired** or **Fast and Wiggly**.

Tip: It is better to do fewer movements with good "form" (keeping your back straight, holding up your body well), than more movements without being able to hold up your body well!

Slow and Tired   Fast and Emotional   Fast and Wiggly

CROSS-CRAWL

Stand with feet planted on the floor. Bring one elbow and its opposite knee together *slowly*.

By doing this you are **crossing midline** (remember that?), when one body part crosses to the other part of the body. This movement causes one side of your brain to talk to the other side, which helps you focus when you need to.

This exercise also provides **proprioceptive input** to your belly, back, arms, and legs, so can make you feel **Just Right**, especially when you are feeling **Slow and Tired** or **Fast and Wiggly**.

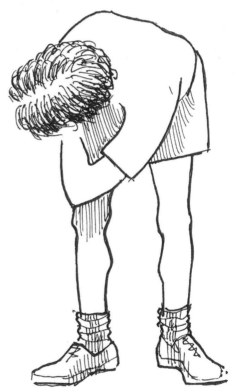

Slow and Tired

Fast and Emotional

Fast and Wiggly

SUPERMAN POSE

Lie on your belly on the floor. Extend your arms in front of you, and hold them straight out. Extend your legs behind you and hold them straight out. Great, you look like Superman! Now hold this pose for ten seconds.

Again, I feel like I am starting to sound like a broken record but this pose also provides **proprioceptive input** to your belly, back, arms, and legs, so can make you feel **Just Right** whether you are feeling **Slow and Tired**, **Fast and Emotional**, or **Fast and Wiggly**.

*Tip: You can also cross your right and left arms in front of you and hold them in position. By doing this you are **crossing midline** (remember that?), when one body part crosses to the other part of the body. This movement causes one side of your brain to talk to the other side, which helps you focus when you need to.*

Slow and Tired   Fast and Emotional   Fast and Wiggly

JUMPING JACKS

The trick to this exercise is to make sure that your arms and legs are moving together. This is what I tell the kids I work with: "Make an X, make an I."

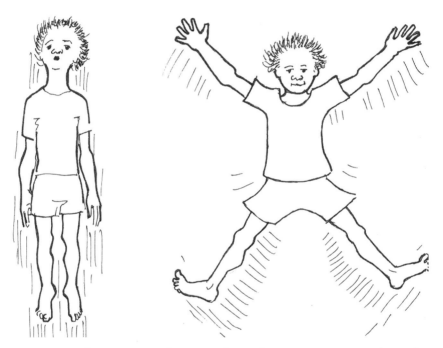

This pose provides **proprioceptive input** to your hands, arms, feet, and legs, so it can make you feel **Just Right**, especially when you are feeling **Slow and Tired** or **Fast and Wiggly**.

*Tip: Remember, do this exercise quickly (but in a controlled way!) if you are feeling **Slow and Tired**. Do this exercise slowly if you are feeling **Fast and Emotional** or **Fast and Wiggly**.*

Slow and Tired   Fast and Emotional   Fast and Wiggly

TAKING SPACE

This is not a *physical* break, but I thought that this was a *super-important strategy* and thought about where to put it. I didn't want to put it with the **Anywhere Body Break** appetizers because you can't do this *everywhere* and you shouldn't need it often. I did not want to put this with the **tools** main courses because I did not want to place it with strategies that should be used as a next step from **Anywhere Body Breaks**.

Instead, I thought that here, with the **Big Body Break** dessert choices would be its perfect home, because needing to take actual space away from friends, classmates, family and community members is something that is not for everyone and not for every situation.

Taking space is when you feel like you need time away safely from a situation that makes your body or mind feel bad. You always need to get permission from an adult to take space, and this must be done in a safe manner, where grown-ups know exactly where you are and for how long you will be there.

Slow and Tired

Fast and Emotional

Fast and Wiggly

Tip: You can even set up a safe spot in your classroom and/or your house. You can ask to put in tools or items that make you feel safe: for example, special fidgets, a weighted lap pad, noise-reducing headphones, markers/paper, a picture of family/friends. This can always be a safe spot for you to go when you begin to feel **Fast and Emotional**, or even **Fast and Wiggly**.

CHAPTER 5

Choosing the Right Strategy is Like Ordering Fast Food...Sort Of

OK, let's review.

1. We have learned what each feeling means.

2. We know that it is normal to experience each and probably all of those feelings in any given day (remember, even your teachers and parents do, too!).

3. We now understand how to utilize strategies and tools from the **Anywhere Body Breaks**, **tools**, and **Big Body Break** choices in order to feel in control of ourselves.

Here's what's just as important as choosing the right strategy: using the strategy or tool the right away. Let's explore that further.

Before we begin, I want you to think of all of the strategies as food options on a menu.

Would you order chicken nuggets if you were really in the mood for pizza?

Maybe you would, if your friends were ordering them, or if you were looking at the menu really quickly. But guess what? Your body would not feel satisfied, because you were really craving pizza! Not the best choice, huh?

Guess what? It's the same thing with these body break/strategy menu choices!

Don't choose an exercise or strategy because you think it looks "the coolest" (trust me, they are all cool—I put them in this book, didn't I?), or because you rushed through reading the choices instead of thinking which strategy your body is most craving or in the mood for.

These strategies work if you *choose which exercises feel Just Right* and you *do them the right way.*

It is important to remember to do these breaks at the right speed (not too fast, not too slow) and with a good amount of pressure. Let's go back to the pizza versus chicken nuggets example.

I promise: We are not just talking about food! (Even though it *did* get your attention, didn't it?)

Scenario 1

I chose to get pizza. Great! That is what my body was in the mood to eat! I want to go play video games with friends, so I rush through eating it, and I do not feel like my craving for pizza was satisfied. I am still hungry, and now I have a stomach ache.

How this applies to us

I look through my sensory manual, and carefully choose to do a **Finger Pull** exercise. That is great, because I have had a really bad day because I spilled my chocolate milk that I just bought from the store all over my books, and now I am late to class. I know that I should stop and do a **Finger Pull** the right way, but I am already late. My friends are walking around the hallway and looking at me. Pushing my books into the crook of my elbow, I hurriedly pull my fingers together for one second, and rush to class. Now, I feel **Fast and Emotional**, and to be honest, probably even more than I did previously, because I did a **Finger Pull** *too quickly*!

Solution

I should have gone to class, and put my books down first. Since this is an **Anywhere Body Break** from our appetizer menu, I can do this strategy *anywhere*. Once I am sitting in class, I can do this exercise with better focus and really put my feelings into my **Finger Pull**. My friends were probably not looking at me. It often *feels* that people notice when I am **Fast and Emotional**, but really, that is usually not the case.

Scenario 2

I am feeling **Fast and Wiggly**, so I read through the menu really fast. I choose to get chicken nuggets. When it comes, I eat it, but leave a lot of it on the plate because I really was not in the mood to eat it. I think to myself: "Why did I order this, anyway?" I run out of the pizza store, my mother yelling at me to slow down before I trip and hurt myself. As I am running, I wonder: "What am I in the mood for—I'm still hungry! I wish I knew."

How this applies to us

My body feels like a jack-in-the-box. My teacher reminds me, "Go choose a strategy from the sensory manual, please." Pushing into chairs, friends, and desks, I grab the book off the whiteboard shelf and fling myself to the sensory corner of my classroom. I flip to the **Anywhere Body Breaks** appetizers page, and randomly choose the **Give Yourself a Hug** choice. I throw my arms across my body, give myself a weak hug, and race back to my teacher. "I did it!" I say loudly, barreling back to my seat, stepping over friends' hands, legs, and desks as I do so. "Why did I choose that body break, anyway? That was not the right one," I think to myself later that day, in the quiet of my bedroom. "If I had chosen a good strategy, maybe Ms. Winston would not have made me miss choice time. What did my body need in that moment? I wish I knew."

Solution

It's hard to know what to do in those moments when your body is feeling out of control, whether it's from being **Slow and Tired**, **Fast and Emotional**, or **Fast and Wiggly**. Helpful adults may need to give us gentle reminders to use **tools** that can assist us in knowing what strategies can help us feel just right; that is where this manual comes in. In this situation, when my teacher told me to go get the book, I made a good choice going to the sensory corner. If you do not have a sensory corner in your classroom, maybe ask if you can have a quiet space while reading (example: in the hallway), or even headphones. I should have read the **Anywhere Body Break** appetizer choices carefully, and gone through the exercises carefully, as well. A good first step before doing any body break is taking a deep breath (also known as a **Bubble Breath**). This will automatically slow you down (both physically and emotionally). If I chose an exercise or strategy that did not work (after doing it slowly, carefully, and with good pressure), then maybe it would have been a good next step to try another **Anywhere Body Break** appetizer choice.

CHAPTER 6

Wow! You are a Body Control and Self-Regulation Expert! But Not So Fast, Your Work is Not Done Yet...

Woo-hoo! You have made it to the end of this book. Congratulations! While the information is fresh in your brain, let's summarize what we have learned.

You now know what our **Slow and Tired**, **Fast and Emotional**, and **Fast and Wiggly** feelings are, and how to make good choices for using this book the right way and choosing the right strategies to feel great.

You learned how to do all of the **Anywhere Body Breaks**, **tools**, and **Big Body Breaks** in this manual.

Just remember, look for the helpful symbols next to each **tool** that match each feeling, for a quick reminder of how that

Anywhere Body Break, **tool**, or **Big Body Break** would help.

The paragraphs below will summarize your next steps to keep this information fresh in your mind so you can stay feeling happy, cool, and collected.

Good for you! As I said at the beginning of this chapter, you made it to the end of this book. We have gone through all of the steps to staying happy, keeping cool, and figuring out how to learn what strategies work best no matter what we may be feeling inside.

But, as it says at the beginning of this chapter, your work is not done. Don't just leave this book on the shelf. Don't think, "Well, I read the book, so I know all about exercises and strategies, I'm fine." That, my friends, is where you will make a mistake.

When you are feeling happy, calm, **Just Right**, it's easy to read through this book, and choose which exercise, tool, or strategy seems like it will work. The challenge is this: can you use this book the right way, choose the strategy that is just right, and keep yourself going on your quest to feeling in control? The hardest times to use these strategies are when we are experiencing those feelings the strongest, those **Slow and Tired**, **Fast and Emotional**, and **Fast and Wiggly** feelings.

Here's the good news: you now have the right "fast food" choices to satisfy what your body needs. I *know* you can make the smart choices for yourself, even when you are not feeling so amazing. (And even when you make a mistake, *or two*, *or three.* It's OK, you're a kid. And guess what? Adults make mistakes all the time. Just don't tell the helpful grown-ups in your life that I told you so.)

OK, here's my goal, or really, my wish for you: I want you to keep reading and studying this book, whether it is by yourself, with friends, or with a helpful grown-up (honestly, I hope it is a combination of all three). The more you read through this book and practice these exercises and tools the right way, the more natural using these strategies will become, until, guess what? You are doing them all on your own! You will be one successful grown-up, let me tell you. I hope you will write to me and tell me all about it.

And, of course, keep rockin' and continue to be awesome!

THE END

P.S. Look in the back of this book for super-useful summaries and charts to help make this book *even easier*! Can you believe it? I know!

PART 2
FOR ADULTS

Acknowledgements and Thanks

There are so many people who have helped to make this book a reality. First and foremost, I would like to thank Rachel Menzies, Commissioning Editor at Jessica Kingsley Publishers, for her patience, hard work, and support in the process of making this book a reality. I would like also to thank Victoria Nicholas and Sarah Minty, Production Editors at Jessica Kingsley Publishers, for their dedication and hard work in making my book what it is today. Thank you to Katelynn Bartleson, Marketing Associate at Jessica Kingsley Publishers, for her efforts in terms of marketing and media. Thank you to the rest of the staff at Jessica Kingsley Publishers for believing in this book, its message, and all of the hard work that has been done to support its production.

To the countless parents and their children whom I have treated over the years: thank you for your wisdom, your smiles, your laughter, your tears, and most of all, your trust. I have learnt so much from you, both as a therapist and as a person. You have a special place in my heart.

To the teachers, counselors, physical therapists, occupational therapists, speech therapists, social workers, psychologists, para-professionals, and administrators who I have had the privilege of collaborating with over the years: you are truly amazing. Your professionalism, love for the children you work with, talent, and genuine goodness of spirit is inspirational.

To those parents, caregivers, teachers, therapists, and others who work with children whom I have not had the pleasure of meeting (yet): you are the motivation behind this book. Your kindness, courage, smiles, and support of your children keeps me believing that the world can be just a bit brighter day by day.

Finally, I must thank my family. Joel: thank you for the countless mornings, afternoons, and evenings where you were left to fend for yourself with the children as I holed away furiously typing these pages. This book would not have been possible without your love, support, and endless patience (and not just with the kids!). You are an amazing husband and father, and I can never express how much I appreciate you every single day. Shayna, Yosef, and Lianna: I have had you all young, but you have schooled me quickly, and have been the best teachers I have ever had. You are my three inspirations, and you bring me joy every day. You are each very special and loved forever.

Some Important Tips for My Fellow Parents

As a mom of three young kids who are spaced very closely in age, who also works full time as a pediatric occupational therapist in a school, teaching my own kids (and myself!) at home how to self-regulate, cope, and manage life on a day-to-day basis was crucial (especially when I had two toddlers and one baby, and all three in diapers!). See the picture below of part of my own household sensory corner (which has been a life-saver).

Sensory toolboxes: part of our sensory corner at home

I believe that *the earlier* children learn to self-regulate and cope with emotional and sensory processing difficulties, *the easier* it is for them to internalize these strategies, and the *better-adjusted* they are as they mature. Both typically developing children and children with different needs can benefit from the implementation of these strategies.

Many of the strategies and tools in this book can be adjusted depending on the age of your child or children. I have taught my kids at home how to use all of these exercises and tools, but have had to make adjustments to specific choices depending on their developmental level.

You are a crucial partner in assisting your child to learn the exercises in this manual. Here are a few simple tips:

- Read through this book for the first time with your child when he or she is feeling calm and alert.

- Depending on the age and focus-capability of your child, you may want to break up your reading of this book into chapters (for example, one chapter a day before bed). Each chapter offers a short summary of the chapters before, so this affords you with the opportunity to discuss and review what has been learned with your child. It is here that you can determine if you need to go back and review a previous chapter, or part of a chapter.

- There are sections of this book with a lot of words, examples and content. If you feel like these sections are too advanced for your child's age level, try summarizing it and connecting it to the corresponding picture.

- Try to obtain a copy of this book for your child's classroom, the place where they spend a substantial portion of their day. The school is a setting in which so many amazing events that shape your child's life happen. It is also a setting where the inevitable academic, social, behavioral, and sensory issues may occur. Our kids work hard! Having a copy in the classroom for your child will allow them to further develop these skills within the context of their peers.

- Have this book as part of a "Sensory Tool Box" or sensory corner in your house (this will be discussed later in the book). Once your child is familiar with the book and how to use it correctly, you can cue him or her to go and find the book, and to choose a strategy, exercise and/or tool that can help them feel "**Just Right**" if they are having difficulty.

- In Appendix 4—At a Glance: Resource Charts, I have created a simple "menu" of all of the different **Anywhere Body Breaks**, **tools**, and **Big Body Breaks**, with simple visual symbols connecting each strategy to specific situations in which they can be most useful. All charts in the appendix section with a 🖥 symbol are available to be downloaded from www.jkp.com. You can photocopy these and laminate them to bring along with you wherever you go, especially if you are traveling somewhere that you anticipate your child may have difficulty. There are a ton of other charts that you can utilize to help reinforce skills and strategies learned in this book, so please see the back of the book for details.

I hope that you and your child enjoy reading this book, and become even closer as a result. You are your child's best therapist and teacher; as a mom and a therapist, I realize how true that is. Utilizing this book consistently is one way that you can help your child stay in control of their body, feelings, and corresponding actions. I am always in awe of fellow parents' love, devotion, and dedication to enriching their children's lives, and as a pediatric occupational therapist, I want to thank you for all that you do for your children.

Note: This book, and all of the strategies provided, are not intended to provide medical or diagnostic information. This book is not a replacement for occupational therapy, physical therapy, vision therapy, speech therapy, or any other specific services your child may need. If your child has a suspected or diagnosed medical condition, speak with your pediatrician before engaging in any suggested exercises, or trying any tools or strategies, to ensure that they are safe and appropriate.

My Delicious Kiddos

Hearing my son, who is visually impaired and can become frustrated by many activities that rely on vision (which unfortunately, is most everything), tell me the other day, while building Lego, that he was feeling **Fast and Emotional** and was going to take a **Bubble Breath** and keep trying made me literally lift him up and do "the happy dance" together. That small moment has become one of increasingly more small yet spectacular self-regulatory victories for my son; and that, dear readers, is my wish for your own children.

Yosef, my four-and-a-half-year-old "little professor," has low vision and is very sensitive to sunlight. See the transition lenses? He usually wears a baseball hat outside but I took it off for the picture. He is doing a **Bubble Breath** exercise from the **Anywhere Body Breaks** appetizer menu here at the park. This exercise is one of his favorites, and really helps calm him down in situations that make him feel nervous or over-loaded (due to his vision issues, he is overly-sensitive to many types of sensory inputs).

As my mother likes to say about my now three-year-old little diva, Lianna was born with a permanent scowl on her face and a scream in her lungs. For the first few months of her life, Lianna spent every day, from 4pm until

11pm screaming her little lungs out inconsolably with little to no reprieve. I read through all of the parenting books over and over, hoping to glimpse the secret to her distress. I bought the expensive formulas. I tried all of my sensory and self-regulatory tricks. Nothing worked—that is, until she was around six months old. Her doctor was convinced that it was colic. I was convinced that I did not care; I just wanted to sleep for more than 30 minutes at a time. Well, she grew from a very demanding baby into a dramatic but adorable little girl. We are working on building her frustration tolerance. She loves going into our sensory corner at home when she becomes angry (hey, it beats going to her room, right?). She is learning to stop and count to ten before getting angry (see below).

I count myself lucky that I have such a sweet and self-aware kid for a daughter. Shayna is only five and a half, but I am sure that she will grow up and go into a helping profession. She is the first to offer advice to her younger siblings when they are having a hard time ("Yosef, why don't you try a **Finger Pull**?"). Lately, she is going through typical little-girl bursts of pushing boundaries moments. When she becomes upset or frustrated, she likes to go to our sensory tool box (located in our kitchen), and put a weighted lap pad across her legs. She will usually go on to continue reading or playing, and is back to herself in a few minutes.

Some Important Tips for Teachers

First of all, I have to tell you that I am a total die-hard occupational therapist. I have an "I am An OT Chick" mug, OT shirts, and OT pins (see the picture below). I am so passionate about what I do, because I was a kid who had a lot of the difficulties that I now work to treat, so I really feel for the kids that I work with and understand (I hope) what can work.

I have to say that I have so much admiration for what *you* do. I work with a group of amazingly talented teachers at the school where I treat, and I am reminded on almost a daily basis of the immeasurable amount of work, love, dedication, and responsibility that you shoulder when you come in to work each day.

I love to work with great teachers, and this collaboration has become a bigger and bigger part of my job as the years go on. Why? Kids spend a large portion of their day in the classroom with their peers, and giving teachers tools, strategies, and tips for their students tends to be a very effective way to manage difficult behaviors and needs.

So, where does this manual come in? This book can be introduced to a whole class, to a group of students exhibiting similar difficulties, or to an individual student. I love the idea of teaching this manual as an approach to more independent self-regulation to the entire class, and having the book as a classroom resource as you are teaching, as well as integrating these strategies into your classroom routines.

Here are some tips to make the most of this manual:

- Read through this book with your students for the first time when they are feeling calm and alert. It may be a good idea to do a self-regulatory whole-class body break (from the **Anywhere Body Breaks** section).

- **Anywhere Body Breaks** are great body breaks to use as whole-class breaks on the rug, or at desks. They can be used as stress-busters before an exam, or after difficult transitions (for example, lunch, recess, or gym).

- It is a great idea to create a sensory tool box for the entire class. This can be placed either in a sensory corner (see the **Big Body Breaks** section) or close to the rug. In my treatment room at school, I break down sensory tool boxes into three separate boxes:

  1. "Fidget Box": holds fidgets (for example, squeeze balls and other small manipulatives).

  2. "Big Tools" box: for larger sensory tools (for example, weighted lap pads, weighted vests, desk correl, headphones, etc.).

  3. "Feelings Books" box: holds books that address socio-emotional, behavioral, and sensory difficulties.

- You can incorporate this book as part of this "Feelings Books" box in the sensory corner in your classroom. Once your students are familiar with the book and how to use it correctly, you can cue them to reference the book, and to choose a strategy, exercise and/or tool that can help them feel **Just Right** if they are having difficulty.

- In the appendix section of this book, I have created a simple "menu" of all of the different **Anywhere Body Breaks**, **tools**, and **Big Body Breaks**, with simple visual symbols connecting each strategy to specific situations in which they can be most useful. There are many other visual charts that work to reinforce learned skills and strategies taught in this book, which can help develop positive self-regulation, emotional regulation, and behavioral reinforcement. All charts in the appendix section with a 🖥 symbol are available to be downloaded from www.jkp.com. You can photocopy these and laminate them to bring along with you wherever you go, especially if you are traveling somewhere that you anticipate a few students may have difficulty (for example, loud assembly, gym, or a class trip).

- There are sections of this book with a lot of words, examples, and content. If you feel like these sections are too advanced for your students, try summarizing it and connecting it to the corresponding picture.

- Depending on the age and maturity level of your students, you may want to break up your reading of this book, based on your students' level of focus. Each chapter offers a short summary of the chapters before, so this affords you the opportunity to discuss and review what has been learned with your students.

I feel truly excited to introduce this into the educational community, because my hope is that it will foster an even stronger collaboration between students, teachers, parents, therapists, and administration. My goal in writing this book is to take another step towards all of us working as a cohesive educational team, as well as between the home and the school settings, to best benefit our students and their families.

I have to say it again, teachers, you are rock stars! Keep doing all the great work that keeps you so memorable in the minds and hearts of the therapists, parents, and most importantly, children, who work with you.

Some Important Information about the Major Sensory Systems

Kids are constantly bombarded with sensory stimuli throughout the day, wherever they are. During school hours, peers play and interact loudly (and sometimes wildly!) in the courtyard and the lunchroom, classrooms are often visually stimulating (with colorful and sometimes cluttered charts and posters on walls and hanging from ceilings), and students are many times in close physical proximity to each other, whether it is at their desks, in line, or on the rug. When children are at home or participating in activities outside school, they must continue to process a continuous wave of sensory stimuli, whether it is when they are crossing a loud and crowded street, playing with friends at an arcade, or even going to the movies.

Children who have no difficulty processing sensory input are able to: take in all sensory information, filter out irrelevant information, and stay relatively calm and self-regulated. They may engage in occasional compensatory behaviors to remain so, such as biting their nails, playing with objects, getting a drink of water/going to the bathroom (when they don't need to), tapping their legs, fidgeting with their hands, etc.

Children who have difficulty processing sensory information effectively have trouble completing school and home-based tasks requiring them to sit still, attend to instruction, be able to engage socially with peers, and play/work cooperatively with others. Sensory input is not processed effectively, so they have difficulty interacting with their environment (and peers) functionally, as they are not receiving appropriate sensory feedback. They may be observed to engage in maladaptive behaviors; for example, they may fidget while seated, put objects in their mouth, and/or have difficulty following multi-step directions (among other difficulties). Providing the child with increased input to a certain sensory system may help improve behavior and overall self-regulation.[1]

Let's now get into a (very) brief overview of the major sensory systems.

---

1   If you believe that your child has a true sensory integrative or self-regulatory dysfunction, please consult with your pediatrician, local occupational therapist or school-based support team, in order to determine whether an occupational therapy evaluation would be appropriate for your child.

The Proprioceptive System

The proprioceptive system is responsible for the individual's sense of where they are in space. Proprioceptive receptors are located in the muscles, tendons, and joints. These receptors respond to both movement and gravity (especially active movement, which is initiated by the child). Providing a child with **proprioceptive input** is a powerful tool to help them self-regulate, especially if you are unsure how they are feeling; that is, it can work whether they are feeling **Slow and Tired**, **Fast and Emotional**, or **Fast and Wiggly**.

Children who have dysfunction relating to the proprioceptive system may have difficulty with:

1. Motor planning, including coordinating and grading their movements.

2. Gross motor activities.

3. Regulating activity levels: that is, they seem to be hyperactive, and seek that deep pressure in ways that may be unsafe (i.e. crashing into walls, jumping off high surfaces, etc.).

4. Appropriate play with peers: they may play aggressively with peers.

5. Behavior: they may engage in self-stimulatory behaviors geared at eliciting that deep-pressure input (i.e. head-banging, biting, pinching, etc.).

6. Postural control, and may exhibit low muscle tone.

The Vestibular System

The vestibular system provides the individual with information regarding the position of their head and body in relation to the ground. The vestibular receptors are located in the inner ear, and are activated by changes in head position and movement (both acceleration and deceleration). Types of movement include linear (i.e. side to side, back and forth, up and down), and rotational.

Children who have dysfunction relating to the vestibular system may have difficulty with:

1. Coordinating smooth and accurate movements.

2. Balance and upright posture.

3. Feeling safe when feet or body is off the ground (also called "gravitational insecurity").

4. Controlling eye movements (including focusing on objects, shifting gaze, tracking, etc.).

5. Maintaining appropriate muscle tone (especially extensor tone).

6. Bilateral coordination skills (utilizing both sides of the body in a coordinated manner).

The Tactile System

The tactile receptors are located in the skin, and detect temperature, movement, light touch, vibration, and temperature. Some parts of the body are more sensitive to tactile input, including the mouth, and palms and soles of the feet. The tactile system is comprised of two components: **protective** and **discriminative**. Tactile discrimination relates to the ability to understand differences in tactile sensations (i.e. vibration versus light touch versus deep pressure).

Children who have dysfunction relating to the protective component of the tactile system may have difficulty with:

1. Perceiving pain.

2. They may demonstrate "Tactile Defensiveness": when a child becomes overly focused on the presented tactile input (because they cannot filter or inhibit it). Since they cannot process this input effectively, the child then reacts with a "fight or flight" response; this response includes difficulty regulating emotions, and appearing as hyperactive. Kids who present with tactile defensiveness may avoid everyday activities and sensations that his or her peers may participate in and actually enjoy (e.g. running in grass, completing art projects, etc.). This may impact their social interactions, as the physical proximity to them may be difficult due to fear of light touch and touch initiated by others. He or she may still crave deep pressure as a type of tactile input which may help to regulate the tactile system.

Children who have dysfunction relating to the discriminative component of the tactile system may have difficulty with:

1. Playing with toys or classroom tools appropriately (since they may have difficulty grading the force of their hand movements).

2. Knowing the property of an object by using touch alone ("stereognosis"), thus relying on the visual system.

3. Localizing pain.

4. Fine motor coordination tasks and skills. This is not due to a motor coordination issue, but rather due to the child not receiving adequate tactile feedback in the hands.

Tips of the Trade! Ways to Make Your Home or Classroom Most Conducive to Self-Regulated Kids

- If you are in doubt about what type of strategy to utilize (e.g. the child is unable to state how they are feeling, or you cannot figure out their self-regulatory state based on your own observations), you can always go with **proprioceptive input**. It is the most powerful and reliable type of sensory input you or your child/student can use. The **proprioceptive system** is most activated through the child's active movement, so think: **hand massage**, **arm massage**, **seat push-up**, **firm fidget**, etc. If that is not possible, passive **proprioceptive input** is always fine (**weighted lap pad**, **weighted vest**, joint compressions—see below).

- *Joint compressions:* This is a form of deep pressure/proprioceptive input that you can provide for your child/student if they are having significant difficulty self-regulating. This is how I do it in my own clinical practice: using two hands firmly (but not too hard!) apply pressure at the shoulders. I move down to the wrists, fingers, knees, and ankles. Make sure to always ask before doing this, especially if a child demonstrates any type of tactile sensitivity. A modified way to provide deep pressure input is to do the **Arm Massage** exercise in the **Anywhere Body Breaks** appetizer menu, replacing the child's hands with your own.

- For children who demonstrate any of the following: tactile hypersensitivity, poor body awareness, impulsivity, or difficulty with personal space, try placing bright painter's tape around the boundaries of their rug spot and/or desk space. Start off with it being larger than it needs to be. Praise them for staying within its boundaries. As their body control improves, slowly make the boundaries of their space smaller as body control and awareness improves.

- For children who have difficulty with transitions, completing **Big Body Breaks** outside the classroom (for the school setting) or in an area that is far from the family (for the home setting) may be too difficult.

Instead, why not set up an area within the classroom or family area as a designated "Big Body Break Space"? For children who have difficulty settling down to complete the exercise, photocopy the "Lauren's Self-Regulation Menu of AWESOME Big Body Break Dessert Choices" page from the book and tape it to the wall as a visual cue for choices and body position.

- Dim lights are calming, and can reduce visual inattention. Consider using natural or incandescent lighting instead of fluorescent lighting.

- Soft classical music in the background during homework or class work/activities can have a calming and self-regulating affect on all children.

- To improve transitions (whether you are in the classroom, or at home—getting on PJs for bed!), consider utilizing one calm song (it can have vocals). Utilizing this during all transitions can improve motor planning, organization, and time management skills.

- For the classroom—try to avoid hanging objects from the ceiling, as they can be very visually distracting to children who are over-stimulated by visual information.

- For children who have difficulty transitioning between activities, consider using a visual schedule. This will allow the child to understand what is expected of him or her, and eliminate potential surprises. Children who can anticipate what to expect throughout the day often have an easier time self-regulating.

- Social Stories™ (The Gray Center)—this is a simple, relevant story that is created to explain a situation, skill, or concept. It shares accurate social information. Creating a Social Story around a situation of difficulty may be a beneficial way to target specific behavior, ease anxiety around a particular event, or reinforce or improve routine adaptive habits, social skills, and self-regulation. You can find out more about Social Stories™ at www.thegraycenter.org.

- I often create my own pseudo-social stories for my three kids at home and the children whom I treat that don't meet every criteria for a formal social story, but are very effective. I recently wrote my daughter a mini social story that is part of our sensory corner's book bin: "Lianna Can Sleep Nicely."

- Utilizing visual timers (e.g. a Time Timer) during non-preferred tasks often improves a child's attention and motivation to complete what is presented, as they have a visual representation of how long they are expected to work. Pair specified work periods (utilizing the timer) with a two to three minute break period using this manual, allowing the child to choose from the **Anywhere Body Break** appetizers, **tool** main dishes, or **Big Body Break** dessert menu choices. Offering the child a sense of control over their breaks should improve attention to task, self-regulation, and motivation to complete what is asked of him or her.

- If you notice that your child/student looks sleepy or unfocused, have them engage in any movement break (**Anywhere Body Break** or **Big Body Break**) that crosses midline. This allows the two hemispheres of the brain to talk to each other, and thus, improve focus. Examples are: **Arm-Pretzel**, **Give Yourself a Hug**, **Cross Crawls**.

- If you see your child is often touching objects in their environment, but tends to throw the fidgets you have given them, try this: attach a fidget or squeeze ball to a keychain, and clip it onto their belt. Another option: Velcro under the desk, under the chair, or even on the floor (they can't throw that!).

- A cheap version of compression vests: try buying tight active-wear shirts and shorts. Their neoprene material provides great compression at a fraction of the cost.

- To improve your child's motivation to want to wear compression and weighted items, have them decorate them with fabric markers. I have had kids decorate their compression clothing and weighted vests with Superman, Batman, Pokémon, and, trust me, they feel like superheroes whenever they wear them.

Readers have permission to download the following pages marked with a 🖥 symbol from www.jkp.com/catalogue/book/9781849059978/resources for your own use at home.

I Caught You Calm!

This chart can improve your child/student's willingness and motivation to utilize strategies, breaks, and tools learned throughout this book by combining independent and efficient use (that is, the utilization of the strategy yielded a positive and observable change in their behavior) with a pre-determined token reinforcement. "Catch" your child or student calm and engaging in these strategies, and even the star cut-out (on page 94) combined with your praise and enthusiasm should yield positive results! Examples of a token reinforcement can be as simple as five extra minutes on the playground, or a trip to the ice cream store!

You will need:

 ★ Velcro dots    ★ Ziploc Bag

★ Scissors

To get the most use out of this chart, laminate it or cover it with contact paper. Cut out the **Anywhere Body Breaks**, **tools**, and **Big Body Break** choices on page 94. Put the squares into a Ziploc bag, and place the Ziploc bag in a place that is easily accessible. Put soft or scratchy Velcro dots on the back of the cut-out **Anywhere Body Breaks**, **tools**, and **Big Body Breaks**. Put three to five dots of the opposite texture on the chart, next to the items: **Body Break/Tool Choices**, and **Stars**. (So if you put scratchy dots on the back of the **Anywhere Body Breaks**, **tools**, and **Big Body Breaks** cut-outs, place soft dots on the chart). Make a collaborative decision with your child/student regarding which strategy/exercises he or she feels would be most effective in keeping them feeling **Just Right**. Place the chart in a visible location, as a reminder to them not only about what strategies to use, but also the progress they have made in terms of how many stars they have earned and the reward they are working towards.

Alternative: If you do not want to cut out all of the strategies, and you feel like the child can simply follow a written or drawn visual next to the labeled items, drawing the strategies and stars on the laminated chart can work just as effectively!

I Caught You Calm!

I Did Body Breaks and Used Tools to Make Myself Feel Just Right ON MY OWN!

Child: _____ **Reward:** _____

Body Break/Tool/Strategy Choices:

Stars:

Child: _____ **Reward:** _____

Body Break/Tool/Strategy Choices:

Stars:

Anywhere Body Breaks (Pictures):

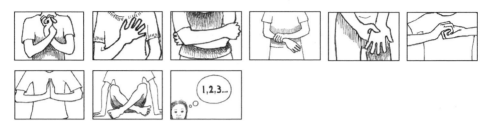

Tools (Pictures):

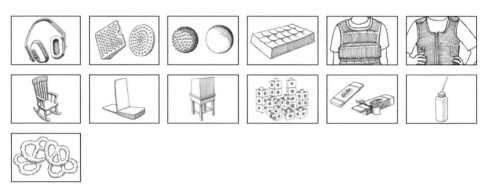

Big Body Breaks (Pictures):

Stars:

Self-Monitoring Checklist

Directions for use: This tool further helps kids label their feelings, and then provides them with a way to act on them. It uses the language learned in this manual and reinforces it through quick visuals. You can laminate the pages provided, punching a hole through them and clipping them together for improved durability and easy access; additionally, if you laminate the pages, your child can write on them, and re-use them over and over again. Make sure to look out for symbols to give you a clue for how these strategies can help!

Lauren's Self-Regulation Menu of AWESOME Anywhere Body Break Appetizer Choices

Anywhere Body Break	Picture	Choice (Check Off as many as you need to feel Just Right)
Arm-Pretzel		
Bubble Breath		
Give Myself a Hug		
Arm Massage		
Hand Massage		
Finger Pull		
Palm Push		
Seat Push-Up		
Count to Ten	1,2,3...	

Did You Use Your Tools the Correct Way? Circle the **Just Right** Check Once You Do! ✓

Do You Feel **Just Right**? Circle the **Just Right** Smiley Face When You Do!
☺

Lauren's Self-Regulation Menu of AWESOME Tool Appetizer Choices

Tool	Picture	Choice (Check Off as many as you need to feel Just Right)
Noise-Reducing Headphones		
Cushion (Wedge or Disc)		
Fidget (Textured or Firm)		
Weighted Lap Neck Pad		
Weighted Vest		
Compression Vest/Clothing		
Rocking Chair		
Back Jack Chair		
Desk Correl		

cont.

Tool	Picture	Choice (Check Off as many as you need to feel Just Right)
Manipulatives		
Gum		
Water Bottle with a Straw		
Crunchy Snacks/Sour or Spicy Flavors/Cold or Frozen Foods		

Did You Use Your Tools the Correct Way? Circle the **Just Right** Check Once You Do! ✓

Do You Feel **Just Right**? Circle the **Just Right** Smiley Face When You Do!
☺

Lauren's Self-Regulation Menu of AWESOME Big Body Break Dessert Choices

Big Body Break	Picture	Choice (Check Off as many as you need to feel Just Right)
Wall Push		
Army Crawl		
Crab Walk		
Cross-Crawl		
Superman Pose		
Jumping Jacks		
Taking Space		

Did You Use Your Tools the Correct Way? Circle the **Just Right** Check Once You Do! ✔

Do You Feel **Just Right**? Circle the **Just Right** Smiley Face When You Do!
☺

Label That Feeling! Pocket Chart

Directions for use: This tool further helps kids label their feelings, and then provides them with a way to act on them. It uses the language learned in this manual and reinforces it through quick visuals. This tool is small, so can be easily put into a child's pocket throughout the school day (especially times of difficulty, such as recess, lunch, trips to the dentist or other less structured and high-level sensory times). You can laminate it for improved durability; additionally, if you laminate this card, your child can write on it, and re-use it over and over again.

Label That Feeling!

I Am Feeling...	Slow and Tired	Fast and Emotional	Fast and Wiggly
I Need...	An **Anywhere Body Break**	A **Tool**	A **Big Body Break**
I Need...	Help From a Grown-up	To Use My Words	Other:
I Need...	Medical Help	My Sensory Manual	Other:

At a Glance: Resource Charts

So, sometimes as a helpful grown-up (whether you are a family member, teacher, or therapist), having a "cheat sheet" is not only helpful but necessary, whether you have one or ten children, and they are having difficulty regulating their bodies, emotions, or both. Using the "Some Important Information about the Major Sensory Systems" section should give you more information to help you determine whether your child is feeling: **Slow and Tired**, **Fast and Emotional**, or **Fast and Wiggly** (or a combination!). Through consistent use of this manual, your child should become a better judge of their own regulation states. Until then, use these quick-tip sheets to assist you to help get your child to feel **Just Right** and in control!

At a Glance: Slow and Tired

Arm-Pretzel		Bubble Breath	
Give Myself a Hug		Arm Massage	
Hand Massage		Palm Push	
Seat Push-Up		Cushion	
Fidget (Textured or Firm)		Gum (especially minty flavors)	
Back Jack Chair		Crunchy Snacks/ Sour or Spicy Flavors/Cold or Frozen Foods	
Water Bottle With a Straw		Cross-Crawl	
Compression Vest/Clothing		Crab Walk	
Army Crawl (especially crossing arms)		Wall Push	
Superman Pose (especially with arms crossed)			

At a Glance: Fast and Emotional

Bubble Breath		Give Myself a Hug	
Arm Massage		Hand Massage	
Finger Pull		Palm Push	
Seat Push-Up		Count to Ten	1,2,3...
Firm Fidget		Lap Pad	
Compression Vest/Clothing		Weighted Vest	
Manipulatives		Gum	
Water Bottle with a Straw		Taking Space	
Rocking Chair		Army Crawl	
Superman Pose		Wall Push	

At a Glance: Fast and Wiggly

Arm-Pretzel		Give Myself a Hug	
Bubble Breath		Arm Massage	
Hand Massage		Finger Pull	
Palm Push		Seat Push-Up	
Count to Ten	1,2,3...	Cushion	
Firm Fidget (or Velcro)		Lap Pad	
Weighted Vest		Compression Vest/Clothing	
Rocking Chair		Manipulatives	
Gum		Water Bottle with a Straw	
Taking Space		Wall Push	
Army Crawl		Superman Pose	
Crab Walk		Cross-Crawl	

Sum it Up Page

This is a quick-reference guide that can be photocopied and placed in a calm-down area, in a homework or classroom work area, or anywhere that you want a child to have quick reminders of major points learned from this manual.

Sensory Manual "The Kid's Guide" Page

1. You always start with **Anywhere Body Breaks**. If that's not enough, you try a **tool**. Finally, the last strategy is a **Big Body Break**.

2. **Big Body Breaks** should last no more than two to three minutes. Ask a helpful grown-up if you need help with timing.

3. Fidget Rules: Eyes on your teacher, fidgets always stay in your hand (they are not toys!); textured fidgets wake you up, and firmer fidgets calm you down.

4. These strategies work if you choose which exercises feel **Just Right** and you do them the right way.

5. It is important to remember to do these exercises and strategies the right way (not too fast, not too slow, and with a good amount of pressure). Remember the pizza versus chicken nuggets example!

6. Generally, if you are feeling **Slow and Tired** (and want to wake your body up), your body break movements should be fast and short.

7. Generally, if you are feeling **Fast and Emotional** or **Fast and Wiggly** (and want to calm your body down), your body break movements should be slow and with more firm pressure.

8. The more you do these breaks yourself without reminders, the quicker you'll feel **Just Right**.

9. Always ask an occupational therapist, teacher (or your parent, family member, or other helpful grown-up) if you have any questions about feeling **Just Right**.

Great Therapy Resources and Websites

Fun and Function
POB 11, Merion Station, PA, 19066
Phone: 1800-231-6329 or 1-215-876-8500
Website: www.funandfunction.com

Therapro
225 Arlington Street
Gramingham, MA 01702
Phone: 1800-257-5376
Website: www.theraproducts.com

Pocket Full of Therapy
92 Vanderburg Rd
Malboro Township, NJ 07746
Phone: (732)462-4474
Website: www.pfot.com

Abilitations
PO Box 1579
Appleton, WI 54912
Phone: 1-888-388-3224
Website: www.store.schoolspecialty.com

You can also write to me with questions or comments, and find self-regulation and occupational-therapy-related activities on my community Facebook page: www.facebook.com/TheOtChic.

Recommended Reading

Biel, L. (2014) *Sensory Processing Challenges: Effective Clinical Work With Kids & Teens*, New York: W.W. Norton and Company.

Heininger-White, M. and Wilson, D. (2000) *S'Cool Moves for Learning*. Shasta, CA: Integrated Learner Press.

Gallahue, D. and Ozmun, J. (2006) *Understanding Motor Development: Infants, Children, Adolescents, Adults* (Sixth Edition).Singapore: The McGraw Hill Companies.

Mailoux, Z. and Parham, D. (2005) "Sensory Integration." In J. Case-Smith (ed.) *Occupational Therapy for Children*. St. Louis, MI: Elsevier Inc.

Paper, L. and Ryba, K. (2004) *Practical Considerations for School-Based Occupational Therapists*. Bethesda: The American Occupational Therapy Association, Inc.